The World Is Made Up Every Day

THE INDIA LIST

Alok Dhanwa

The World Is Made Up Every Day

SELECTED POEMS

TRANSLATED BY SAUDAMINI DEO

LONDON NEW YORK CALCUTTA

Seagull Books, 2025

First published in Hindi as *Duniya roz banti hai* by Alok Dhanwa

First published in English translation by Seagull Books, 2025

ISBN 978 1 8030 9 507 3

British Library Cataloguing-in-Publication Data
A catalogue record for this book is available from the British Library

Typeset by Seagull Books, Calcutta, India
Printed and bound by WordsWorth India, New Delhi, India

For Gyanranjan

Contents

Translator's Foreword

An image, not seen, but heard: the city of Delhi in the 1980s, a lane in front of Shastri Bhavan—and an official building whose name one forgets—filled to the brim with people waiting in the rain to hear Alok Dhanwa. He reads to an enchanted crowd, then leaves with a few others for a fellow poet's house in Pushp Vihar, near Saket in South Delhi. On the way, unable to find any bus or auto rickshaw in the pouring rain, the group of poets breaks out in songs from old Hindi films. The perennial image of the poets walking along India Gate, loudly singing songs in the rain, now seems both joyful and melancholic. Alok Dhanwa writes in 'White Nights': 'I, too, wanted to find meaning / in being born in India. / But that India no longer exists, / the one in which I was born' (p. 73 in this volume).

Dhanwa, a cult poet of the 1970s and 80s, primarily wrote against the establishment, which made him immensely popular, particularly among Hindi-language readers in his home state of Bihar and neighbouring regions of North India. Even now, working-class people engage with his poetry like long-lost anthems. Unsurprisingly, he remains little published. *Duniya roz banti hai* (The World Is Made Up Every Day), first published in 1998, remained his only book-length collection until recently. His second volume, *Mulaqaatein* (Meetings), appeared in 2023. He has made a living through writing and theatre practice, and has also taught as visiting faculty at several universities. He was writer-in-residence at Mahatma Gandhi International Hindi University, Wardha, and served as the chairman of the Bihar Sangeet

Natak Akademi from 2014 to 2017. He has also worked with various social organisations and NGOs.

Born in 1948 in Munger, Bihar, Alok Dhanwa quickly rose to popularity with his hard-hitting political poems, at a time when leftist and Marxist political movements were at their peak in the country. His first poem 'Janata Ka Aadmi' (Man of the Masses) was published in 1972 in *Vaam Patrika*, a journal of leftist writings. Shortly after this, his second poem 'Goli Daago Poster' (Shoot-the-Bullet Poster), published in the literary magazine *Filhaal*, questioned the rights of the state. It is virtually impossible to detach Dhanwa's *oeuvre* from the politics of India, and having been born a year after the independence of India, it's almost as if he grew up alongside India, witnessing the many nuances of its existence alongside his own.

The backdrop of Dhanwa's poetic life is the volatile period of Maoist and Naxalite movements in India. The term 'Naxalism' is derived from the town of Naxalbari, nestled in the far north of West Bengal, which was the centre of a tribal peasant uprising in 1967. Even though the uprising was quashed, it kindled several other Communist-led secessionist movements in indigenous regions in India—primarily in the Northeast, which later spread to other parts of the country. These movements, sometimes marked by violence, stood against the imperialist actions of the nation-state, which often laid claim to indigenous lands, displacing and marginalizing the original inhabitants of the region. The rise of the leftist movements eventually led to the creation of the Communist Party of India (Marxist–Leninist) in 1969 and to the emergence of other 'rebel' groups such as the Maoist Communist Centre and the Peoples' War Group.

Apart from these movements, the 1970s were particularly tumultuous in the history of modern India, especially with the growing dominance of Indira Gandhi's political persona. The decade was marked by a demand for political representation from large sections of the Indian electorate, to which the Indira Gandhi–led Congress Party responded with an election campaign focused on abolishing poverty and unifying the fractured masses. Congress won the election by a landslide, and Indira Gandhi emerged as a powerful leader, growing increasingly unconcerned with constitutional processes. Although Gandhi's tenure was marked by several leftward-leaning political reforms, including the nationalization of banks and abolition of privy purses of former princely states, it was also a time of increasing authoritarianism that eventually led to the imposition of Emergency: a twenty-one-month period from 1975 to 1977, during which Prime Minister Indira Gandhi suspended constitutional and civil rights, as well as cancelled elections. The period saw the suppression of both right- and left-wing opposition, with prominent activists and politicians across the political spectrum being jailed, and the media either censored entirely or coerced into supporting the government. The following two decades witnessed the end of Congress' hegemony, the assassinations of both Indira Gandhi (1984) and her son and successor Rajiv Gandhi (1991), the collapse of the USSR and the dream of the Soviet utopia, and India's neo-liberal economic reforms, which ushered in a new era.

It is against this backdrop that Dhanwa's poetry must be read, even though many of his poems address themes beyond overt politics, such as the landscape of rural India, its many hues, trees, fruits, and everyday joys. They're as much about class struggle and militant rebellion as they are about love, women's innate desire to escape the confines of their homes, or an afternoon nap under the shade of a tree. In his universe, these things are not mutually exclusive. However, it would perhaps be a mistake to read Dhanwa as a poet of the past. Contemporary Indian milieu is far more complex, with its growing shift towards majoritarian politics and authoritarianism. His lines 'that India no longer exists, / the one in which I was born' hauntingly resonates with the contemporary reader. Or, when he writes: 'Homicide and suicide are made to look alike / in these half-dark times. Do spot the difference, my friend,' (p. 22) it feels as though he is speaking about present-day India. And, perhaps, there is no end to these half-dark times.

At the end of this volume, we are confronted with the inevitable question: What is India? Is it a modern nation-state, or merely a semblance of one? Is a modern nation-state, with all its ideals and egalitarian promises, even possible, or is it inherently unequal? What happens when a person is made to inhabit the idea of nationhood?

In Dhanwa's world, the marginalized are not merely a voiceless entity, witnessing life from the periphery, but are willing to fight for what has been snatched from them. One wonders, though, what the result of this fight will be—but in this universe, there are no final outcomes. It's the struggle that matters, the resistance that must be kept alive.

It's a book that first smoulders, then explodes like a bomb.

The World Is Made Up Every Day

The Mango Tree

Decades old,
this mango tree,
twilight-tinted

Bent to the ground,
some of its branches move upwards,
others move together towards the open,
uplifting the trunk

Under the tree, at night,
warmth like that of hay,
nests, breath of birds,
the scent of their feathers and shit,
shadow like that of black earth

(1996)

The Rivers

Ichamati and Meghna
Mahananda
Ravi and Jhelum
Ganga, Godavari
Narmada and Ghaghara—
it pains to even say their names

I meet them only as much as
they are on the way

And even then,
the mind can only go so close—
the mind is always filled
with the noise of the predatory markets

(1996)

Goats

Had there been thickets in the infinite,
goats would have stopped by too,
nibbled on the leaves, filled their bellies,
and returned to some familiar veranda
on earth

When I first went to the hills,
even on the sharpest ascents
I met goats
they'd climb up
from villages far below,
continuing their ascent,
just as, every summer,
the vegetation disappears from below

But there were no shepherds in sight
perhaps they were dozing
under the shadow of some peepal tree,
only they are blessed with such tranquility

(1995)

Slumber

Night-drifter
stop by my soul too
grant me a sleep
without even the weight of a single straw

A sleep
that resembles water grass on the moon

(1995)

Body

What women created through the ages—

In those nights, bodies grew ever more intimate
now I look for it within my own body

(1995)

Mir

Talking about Mir
is as beautiful
as Mir

And all that you say
in the candour of ardour,
heart-and-heart
repeating the matters of the heart
saying, insisting that your heart,

Janab, is the heart
that has returned from the streets of Mir

(1996)

District Magistrate

You are an uncultured speaker.

You speak in a language of dissent
as if you're defying kings!
A language from a time
when there was no parliament!

What do you think?
Parliament has preserved the language and tools of dissent,
as they were,
from the time of kings?

This man here,
listening to you from across the table,
paying close attention,
is not a king, but a district magistrate!

The district magistrate,
is usually
far more educated than kings,
and far more earnest and enmeshed!

This boy was born in our lanes.
He was not born in a distant fort—in desolate splendour,
but raised in streets like ours.
He grew up amidst our fumbles and failures.

He knows our grit and our greed.
He is more patient and tactful than kings.

He can create more confusion among us,
keep us further from freedom, and do so more efficiently.
We must keep a
strict,
watchful eye
on this brilliant mind of the government!

At times, we may even need to learn from him!

(1989)

What Saved My Soul

What saved my soul?
Light from two-pice candles

A couple or more boiled potatoes

Bonfire of dry leaves,
earthenware,
bed of straw,
and the straw-coloured moon

The young, vagrant street-play actors
wearing tatters,
their voice, honourable as truth,
fiercely fighting,
chasing away the rioters
at every bend,
learning tricks of the stage from brave, defiant Hindustanis,
their performance—nervous, like wet clothes

Holding new tongs, a gift for his grandma,
Little Hamid returning from Eidgah fair.
And after 6th December,

till sometime before February,
the wild jujubes—

saved my soul

(1996)

Desire

What do I have there
where the rivers meet the sea,

I do not know
but one day, I must go there

When I see someone heading that way,
how this desire flares up!

(1996)

Shoot-the-Bullet Poster

Is this the 20th April of 1972,
or the right hand of an assassin, or the leather gloves
of a spy, or a smudge on
an assailant's binoculars?
Whatever it is—I can't call it just another day!

The place where I write
is very old,
where even today
tobacco is used more than words.

Here, the sky is as high as a pig's back
here, the tongue is used the least
here, the eye is used the least
here, the ear is used the least
here, the nose is used the least.

Here are only stomachs and teeth
and hands buried in the soil.
Man is nowhere to be seen,
just a blue void
that keeps asking for food—

From one torrential rain
to another torrential rain.

Is this woman my mother, or
a five-foot-tall iron rod
on which hang a few pieces of stale bread—
like dead birds?
There is no difference, not even by a hair's breadth,
between my daughter and my protest.
While the Constitution,
on its own terms,
keeps crushing both my daughter and my protest.

After these snap elections,
should I stop
thinking of bullets altogether?
On this 20th April of 1972,
will I be able to live
as the father of my children?
Like an inkpot full of ink—
like a ball,
will I be able to live with my children,
in a field full of grass?

Even if they sometimes carry me in their poems,
they blindfold me, use me

and drop me somewhere beyond the border
They never let me reach the capital.
I am apprehended by the time I reach districts-towns.

Not the government—no, it was the country's
cheapest cigarette that stood by me.

Around my sister's feet,
my childhood grew—
like yellow castor flowers,
the inspector's buffalo chewed up
To keep humanity alive,
if an inspector has the right to fire a bullet
Then why don't I?

The land
on which I sit and write this,
the land on which I tread,
the land I plough,
the land where I sow, and
the land from which I harvest grains, haul to warehouses
do I have the right to shoot for that land,
or do those two-faced landlords
who want to turn this country into a moneylender's dog?

This is not a poem,
but a grasp on firing bullets

that those who wield pens
get from
those who wield ploughs.

(1972)

Theatre

There
is no end to
a park bench
it merely rests on the ground,
yet its presence continues outside the city

The lights on the bridges
have no end
My nights are full of them
I will remember
the lights
even in the face of death

The little long-beaked bird, the woodpecker,
I barely glimpsed it
two–three times
in the past ten–twelve years

It will be seen again,
this time in the theatre

There is no end to
a Theatre
Theatre is not the name of a building

(1996)

Awe, Like Watermelon

It started to seem bigger
as I returned from its shores

Now, I see more of the women
who kissed me as a child

The animals
who played with me in distant daylight
not knowing how to wait

And those first umbrellas,
the clouds so close to them

The ocean carried me into that afternoon
when I couldn't even speak
when crying was calling

Where awe,
like watermelon,
is as green as it is red

(1990)

The Light of the First Film

The night the dam broke
and flooded the city

You didn't even ask

As if you grew up
without this city—
the one with your first train
and the light of your first film

(1997)

Difference

You'll see,
one day, I too will step out in the evening
for a while, just like that,
but won't be able to return.

It will be assumed
that I have ended myself.

No, this will be impossible,
a complete lie!
You must not believe it.
You, who know me a little!
You,
who have pinned the red-flag
countless times
on my shirt, next to my heart—
you must not believe it!

Even in your weakest moment
you must not think
my mind has died.
No, never!

Homicide and suicide are made to look alike
in these half-dark times
Do spot the difference, my friend.

(1992)

The Price

Now even forgetting commands a great price

This is what they do now—
the greedy and depraved

(1997)

The Train

Every decent man has a train
that runs to his mother's house,

whistling,
smoke billowing

(1994)

About Myself

The night has been arriving
and leaving for such a long time
on earth

Yet, witnessing the night,
being in it,
feels extraordinary

I mean,
I am talking about myself

(1996)

Seven-Hundred-Year-Old Verse

Which way did the earth turn,
that apples began to bloom

The small-town moons,
I remember each one,
their promises soaring above the rain

Droplets settled on the leaves of grass
scattering in the midst of sleep

Sunlight descending into a lemon

When her first love turned to ash
the dusky dance teacher saved herself
She was later seen in morning marches against the riot—
body and community becoming one

Cutting short her long leave,
she returned to work,
to her students,
to make them practise
a seven-hundred-year-old verse

(1994)

The Colourist

An old car is being painted,
it will be painted to the brim

(1991)

Sunset Skies

So many sunsets, so many skies
their many colours
Evening spreads slowly, ever so slowly,
along the long roads

Lights bloom
around the hotels
Crowds of people—
their faces visible from a distance
their shoulders, familiar voices

Someday, in this country,
poets will write about these
like events

(1996)

Sky-like Winds

Ocean,
your shores are of autumn

And you yourself, Ocean,
are of the sun and salt

Your sound
is one of depth and dissent

And the winds
crossing through many lands,
enter you
like the sky

The desire to cross you
rarely stirs—
the fear of losing one's way lingers

(1994)

Junction

Ah, Junction!
Where trains halt for a long while,
refilling water for the journey ahead

There, I search
for my old companions

(1994)

The Streets

Our streets used to pass through houses,
vast courtyards,
verandas stretching in every direction,
and doors opening into lanes
where sunlight streamed in until day's end

And those trees,
encircled by rooftops in such a way
that we could climb any tree
and land on anyone's roof

The was a time
when we were more monkey than monkeys,
more cat than cats

Just yesterday,
we were there in the streets,
flinging stones at electric poles

(1996)

Autumn Nights

Autumn nights,
so light and open,
as if it's all evening until the morning

And these evenings
would have their nights in another season

(1992)

The Sea and the Moon

When the sea was rising towards the moon
at the farthest edge of western India
That evening, I saw it.

And the moon,
as big as the wheel of a tram,
and that city, Calcutta, so far off,
where the trams run.

The sea was rising towards the moon,
like only horses can,
as if they are seen
only when they're galloping.

The ocean sea was rising towards the moon,
I stood close—
A certain loneliness, a certain anxiety
I even felt like crying,
but couldn't.

And how the night was approaching,
in such towering waves,
that nothing could be seen
except my old shirt.

It was hard to stay there long,
so I came back into Bombay.

(1990)

The Trail

The woods are deep there,
trails winding through them.

A little ahead, a slope begins
descending to the riverbank.
There the women
are cutting grass
while talking among themselves.
From within the deep woods,
their chatter can be heard.

(1996)

The Birds and the Stars

The birds are leaving, and the stars arriving.

A few minutes ago,
my worn-out pants were awash with the sunset.

For a long while,
the grass field ahead kept fading,
its dust rising with my every step.

Damp purple specks fell in my shadow,
scattering incessantly—
as if I should never have come this way.

(1990)

Caravan

The sea and the city
are full of each other's memories.

The ports are their pathways,
and the workers their caravans.

In the evening,
as seafarers drop anchor in deep waters,
the city turns on its lights.
Women appear, standing in doorways.
What thoughts fill their minds,
what kind of land—
It's water above sand,
and water under sand.

When those who work at sea
return to the city,
the night begins.
It's the week of holidays—
a week-long night.
For seven days, there will only be night.
There will be sorrow, but restaurants will stay open,
and films will play on past midnight.

Songs will rise in chorus,
men and women will sing together,
children will join in,
and even the pets.

The ships' anchors will sleep inside the sea.

Then, the next week will be all sea.
But this week, it's all city.

(1997)

Girls on the Rooftops

Even now,
girls come on the rooftops,
their shadows fall upon my life.

As if the girls appear for the boys
playing cards in the lanes below,
on stairways built above the drains
and those sipping tea
on benches by the tea stalls on the footpath,
around a boy sweetly playing
on his mouth organ
the immortal tunes of *Awara* and *Shri 420*.

In front of a newsstand laid out on the street,
young men stand, some are even reading newspapers.
Not all of them students,
some are unemployed, some employed,
a few lafangas too.

But in their blood runs the same anticipation,
the yearning for a woman!
They believe from these houses and rooftops,
one fine evening, love will descend!

(1992)

Chowk

The splendour of those women stayed with me,
who taught me to cross the chowks!

They were from my neighbourhood,
every morning, they'd leave for work.
My school was on their way,
Ma would hand me over to them.
After school, I'd wait for them—
they taught me to wait.

It was my first time attending
a small-town school.
Within a few days,
I began going on my own.
A few more days later,
many boys became my friends
Together, we took other streets,
walking to and from the school.

But even now,
decades after those fleeting days,
whenever I pass through
a chaotic chowk in a big city,
I remember those women

and I extend my right hand
towards them
while holding in my other hand
the slate I left
behind twenty years of newspapers.

(1992)

The Hungry Child

I am not the brain
I am merely the hungry child's intestines!

That child's soul is falling like dew,

like the bamboo shoots cracking in wasteland, rising upwards.
The child's head cranes up, a little higher each week,
the child's arms stretch longer in the air each minute,
the child's skin hardens,
minute by minute, like leaves stiffening
and—
the child's back widens like grass
and
like grass seeps into the entire atmosphere

Yet in that child's bloodstream,
I am not even a dash of smoggy salt.

In that child's bloodstream,
I am only a watery form,
only a water stimulation!

(1973)

Kite

One

From their blood sprout the kite threads
and
they rise into vast streams of air
since birth they bring along strands of cotton.

Whether sunlight soars high like an eagle
or hangs low like a fruit—
Time, like a buzzing lemon,
leaves its juice on their tongue.

The storm comes and goes,
heavy rain falls and fades,
loo wind flays, then fades
but they wait endlessly
for the sun to soften, the sun to soften
the sun to soften, open,
for the days to become gentler,
for the days to become simpler,
so that the delicate world of kites and threads can start over,
the delicate world of children and birds' eyes.

Two

The darkest nights were of the monsoon
the blackest clouds were of the monsoon
fiercest showers of the monsoon
that bend masts, beat nagada
thundered through the land—
Showers that shook wells and ponds
extinguished lanterns and candles.

In such darkness, only Grandma tells
her lengthiest stories
to children awakened by thunderclap
to those petrified birds
that have flown out of trembling bushes,
looking for a dry hole in the wall,
with their wet beaks and feathers!

Birds can live for a long time—
only if you stop killing them.
Children can live for a long time—
if only you stop killing them.
You kill them with hunger,
with epidemics,
with floods and bullets.
You killers of children!
One day, you will be cast out of the world,
oh, you rulers, murderers of children!

Beware!
One day, you will be thrown into ice
where you will rot to death,
and your weapons will rot with you.

Three

The fiercest showers have passed with the monsoon.
Morning breaks—
a crimson dawn, like the eyes of a rabbit.
Autumn arrives, crossing bridges,
riding a shiny new bicycle
ringing its bell loudly,
calling out brightly,
to the children flying kites,
softening the sky,
until the kites begin to rise—
The world's lightest and most colourful things may fly,
the world's thinnest paper may rise,
the world's thinnest bamboo frames may ascend—
and the fragile world of whistles, laughter
and butterflies may begin.
Since birth, they bring along strands of cotton.
Earth spins towards their restless feet
as they run deliriously,
smoothening the rooftops,

playing at both ends like a mridanga.
They leap,
with the lithe swiftness of branches,
to the dangerous edges of rooftops—
The rhythm of their exhilarated bodies
saves them from falling off.
The trembling heights of kites hold them
suspended by the thread.

They, too, are flying with the kites,
breathing through their pores.

If they ever fall from the precarious edges
and survive
they return even bolder, facing the golden sun.
The earth comes spinning faster,
towards their restless feet.

(1976)

Outside the Conch

I am passing through this conch, long as an animal's trunk.
Water axes cleave the conch,
and I cleave the water axes.

Outside the conch, Ma waits,
a tiger's shadow resting on her temple—
her skin cracks with the roar,
and blood, coarse as a coconut rope, oozes out.
Yet she remains my mother, waiting for me.
She does not become solitude, an object, or emptiness.
Since I was born, Ma has never been alone—
and I am passing through this animal trunk-like conch.

Eyebrows singed by sunlight, legs crippled by cold.
Untimely deaths, as solid as iron pellets—hard, heartless.
Deaths everywhere: children's deaths
deaths for want of milk
deaths for want of wheat
Who stops milk from reaching children?
Who withholds the wheat?
Bring out that tyrant!

Outside the conch, Father bends lower and lower,
his spine bowing to the ground

I will never see his back upright again—
not even in poems.
Drinking rice water, chewing corn,
Father is hollowed out.
The zamindar seized all his words,
along with the shimmering rice.

I am a poet? Am I truly a poet?
Or just a paper-cutter
Am I a field,
covered with reams of newspaper?
Outside the conch, guns stand tall.
And around those weapons,
people plough the earth.

(1973)

Water

People, but not just people,
I believed I would teach
even water to inhabit India.

I believed
Water would be simple—
like the East,
like a straw hat,
like candlelight.

In the golden hour,
the other side is barely visible,
leading us to wander
in a country
yet to appear on the map.

Like a flourishing vine at the top,
ascending towards an unknown dome
it would rest in an earthen pitcher
to quench my thirst.

In autumn, it would get thinner,
spotless and slow,
Under the shade of a corner tree on the banks.

I believed
it would serve not only the body.
The night we stayed awake on the boat—
That night, did the water
return only to the bodies, then ebb?

What all did we establish
since we began writing?

I don't know how much speech
we have wasted,
writing of ruin
while being ruined?

Water doesn't merely
follow commands.
While merely hydrating a plant,
how deep does it seep
into that patch of soil?

Do the voices of water
remain in the voices of women?
And what of other voices?

In a sad and broken heart
there is only the night of water.
There lies hope, and there lies
the only path back into the world.

(1997)

Matinee Show

Love
behind old, dilapidated trucks, I have loved
Sometimes even inside them,
making space in the vine-filled trash,
turning the evening into a curtain,
often without lies,
and without the moon

Awadh, Lucknow, was faraway
its alluring tongue, drenched in Rekhta.
For now, there was no country—
except the star at the golden hour
the city behind our backs.
It was and it wasn't a city,
it was yet to become
as it is still being made.

Bastis alive with women and children,
and their endless lanes—
We would leave them behind,
keeping out of their sight.
Embracing the sky
above those half-built walls over footpaths,
we would enter the cinema hall.

In the darkness of the immortal matinee show—
I have loved.

Our education was sparse,
our means of living harsh.
There wasn't enough free time
to argue, to wander until our end
Our bodies, raised in dense crowds,
held chaos and desire.
We remained almost strangers
to the vacant fear
that accompanies love.

As if marriage was our destination,
our way forward.

Eventually, our wedding was finalized.
And then, whenever there was a break
I would take my would-be wife for a spin
on my bicycle, she would sit in front,
and we would ride—
Down some shadowy road,
away from the city—
hiding.
Sometimes together,
we would whistle as I loved.

The family soon agreed—
our hardworking family,
was not so complicated,
not so stone-hearted
that they could watch us die,
again and again.
We were not strangers to them.
Our innocence
was in their blood as well.

So, one day, we were happily married.
Running a household,
visiting neighbours—
We still loved.

There is no need to search for
the newly recruited lovers around here.
Before a month passes, they are famous.
I am always ready to help them—
changing their tyres,
refilling engine oil.

(1996)

A Poem of Another Era

There on the branch, the fruits ripened
and from them, light would spill.

We would run fast
from the field to our home.
Sometimes ahead of us,
and sometimes behind, the rain.

Among the roots of tall grass
little flowers, from another plant,
would bloom.
Those that could be seen
only when one peered into dense grass.

When clouds gathered suddenly,
and evening fell before its time,
Ma would call out for us
walking all the way
to the edge of the village.

If we stayed awake late,
we'd hear many sounds
that could not be heard during the day—

The sound of a bucket dipping into the well,
the heavy breathing of animals,

a lone bird shrieking
among the stars.

At the time of harvest
Father would return home exhausted
and Ma
would talk to him in the sweetest voice.

Black nights were very black.
White nights were very white.

Sujata, my sister's friend,
would sing beside the pond.
There was a curly-haired boy, Diwakar,
who'd secretly listen to her songs.
One day, Sujata left for West Bengal,
Her family went along.
And Diwakar remained in Bihar.

Many people left the village,
never to return.

In the monsoon easterlies,
my sister and I
would wander in the orchard.

She would show me how trees soak in rain—
the leaves dripping,
but the branches within

barely wet.
The fat trunk below,
almost never drenched.
We'd touch the resin on the bark.
The orchard carried a scent everywhere,
a smell we loved.

Whenever Ma wore a new saree,
she'd hum to herself.
We would tease her,
calling her a new bride.
But she wouldn't mind.
She'd give us new jaggery
along with a few peanuts.

When she had some time to spare,
she would tell us stories
from the time when
she was a child.
It was hard to believe
that Ma, too, was once a child.

At dusk, while lighting the lamps,
she would sing.
She liked singing in the evening,
as she lit up the house.
Ma was illiterate,

but she was never short of songs.
Sometimes, she sang us new songs—
perhaps she was one of those nameless village poets.

In the evening light, she'd sing.
We, her children,
huddled close to her body,
listened in silence.
She sang so beautifully,
that we felt
she must do nothing else
but then, she'd have to return to the kitchen.

Shielding the lamp's flame,
from the wind with a corner of her saree,
she'd cross the courtyard.
In the golden dusk, underneath the neem tree,
we'd watch her enter the kitchen.
As the night deepened,
we couldn't bear
to be away from her.

Even now, after all these years,
I haven't forgotten
Ma's songs at dusk.
Under the moonlight,

the falling of wild berries by the riverbank.
I have kept them safe,
sheltered from the storms of sorrow.

(1995)

Runaway Girls

One

Shackles of home
become starkly visible
when a girl runs away.

Does it remind you of the night
replayed ever so often in old films
when a girl fled her home?
Those rain-soaked, stone-cold lampposts,
their light barely enough
to reflect the restless eyes?

And those songs of passion
on the silver screen—
today, they have come true
within your own walls!

Did you believe those songs
were written solely for actors?
And that haunting portrayal
of Laila's ruin—
that rose unceasingly from the screen
seeping into the private lives of the audience?

Two

You will never read aloud
the letter she left behind
on her desk before running away
You will hide from the world
her discourse.
You will steal
her glass, her mercury
her ebony comb,
her seven-masted boat—
But how will you steal
the life a runaway girl.
So much of it could still be hiding
in the twilight folds of her dupatta?

Her remaining things—
will you burn them too?
Will you also burn
her absence,
that reverberates more than her presence—
like santoor
in her hair.

Three

You'll erase her.
You'll erase the runaway girl
from the air of her own home.
You'll even erase her
from the childhood she left within you.
I know
the violence of nobility.

But the fact that she ran away
will not disappear from memory
like old windmills.

She is not the first girl
to run away
neither will she be the last.

Many boys
and many girls
will run away in the month of March.

When a girl runs away
it is as though she vanishes into flowers,
vanishes into stars,

running in a swimsuit
through a crowded, glittering stadium.

Four

If a girl runs away,
it doesn't always mean
a boy has also run away.

There are many other matters
she might pursue.
She could do anything—
Being a woman
is not just about giving birth.

Outside that battle tank–like house of yours,
sealed and guarded,
girls have changed a lot.
I won't let you
peddle away even her possibilities.

She could be anywhere
she could even fall
she might scatter herself
but she will do it all on her own.
She will make her own mistakes,
she will see it all,
from beginning to end.
She will even face her own end.
She will not die someone else's death.

Five

When a girl runs away
as though riding a white horse
across greed and gambling,
from the crumbling grooms—
how much dust rises!

You
who keep your wives apart
from prostitutes,
and lovers
separate from wives—
How terrified you are
when a woman roams fearless,
seeking her own self
among prostitutes, wives
and lovers alike.

By now, she could be anywhere—
in those upcoming countries
where love will be
a full-time occupation.

Six

So many girls
run away in their minds,
in their sleepless nights, in their diaries.
Their numbers far exceed
the girls who actually run away.

Did any girl ever run away for you?

Is there not a single red-soiled trail
in your nights?

Was marriage handed to you?
Did you simply take it,
claiming it with your status, with your power?
Did you just take, at once
all nights of a woman
even those
after her death!

You have never once wept,
embracing a woman.

'Just stay tonight,'
has no woman ever said to you.

'Just stay tonight,'
countless women have said this,
time and again,

the world over,
racing to the edge of the ocean's doors.
'Just stay tonight,'
and for as long as the world remains,
tonight will remain.

(1988)

Canvas Shoes

Beside the sparkling railway tracks,
there are these old canvas shoes.
A man left them behind—
he disappeared after a single step,
for the world of shoes is made of a single step.

The passer-by on that side,
following the single step—
those old canvas shoes.
Rainwater has remained inside those shoes.
When the strong wind blows, the rainwater moves like a foot.

Soaking wet, these shoes are covered in mildew,
on the thinnest layer of soil,
they have begun to sprout.
I can only imagine,
how often, in decisive moments of play,
these shoes must have burned like the sun!
Inside these shoes are scattered
dust-filled, mountainous paths,
the lost shores of sounds and fields which keep them there—
the lost shores of sounds and fields—
outside of human needs.

How many times have
the spirits of wandering travellers descended.
With their feet, inside these shoes—
for months, they must have inhabited
these shoes.
Spirits—
beyond rooftops and nation states—
far above sea level!

These canvas shoes
soft and filled with air
as cigarettes and handkerchiefs.
Woven like nests—
against solid things in this world like murder and rape,
these liquid shoes stand
bending with grass and language,
edging closer to salt—
And for the rats, these canvas shoes are like the alphabet—
it's where they begin to nibble.

Where the world of shoes began,
shepherds must have found their way.
There is a density inside shoes
that cannot be destroyed.
Even in sheep, a quiet density remains,
a place where the ocean can be heard.
And such a density exists—

a space where the seeds of sleep are safe.
Animals, too, must have found their way
to where the world of shoes began.

Shoes—ancient as boats,
even if made just yesterday,
like fruits—
that are more ancient than shoes or boats,
even if ripened last night,
like sails—
which appear more ancient than our clothes.
Yet our clothes
are far more ancient than sails.
Ancientness is something
to cradle in your knees
so they never bow to a tyrant—
for fear is ancient too,
and so are weapons.

And earth—
older than fruit
as ancient as the seed.
Walking on earth
is such a simple task.
Yet, to watch someone walk on earth
is to witness an ancient scene.
Walking on earth is such a simple task

and still,
the memory of walking on land is deep.

Beside the sparkling railway tracks,
they are no longer just old canvas shoes,
rather, they have become
dim, dangerous paths
on which even spies are unable to walk.
But when the stars begin to scatter,
and the branches of evening fill those old shoes—
then, on those dim, dangerous paths,
the distant wheels of dreams come spinning swiftly,
scattering light and roots in someone's sleep,
and gathering, like greenery, those useless,
abandoned, discarded things.

Animals come from nature. And days, too.
But shoes didn't come from nature.
Shoes were made by humans—
just as humans made gardens.
Likewise, humans created great things
to accompany them.
And among those great things,
shoes are the closest to humans—
Closer than boats,
closer than roads, railways and stairs,

like efforts and tunes,
they are constantly seeking entry.

Those canvas shoes are now so old
that one might say,
wherever they move, Time doesn't exist—
even Death would no longer want to wear them.
But poets do wear those shoes,
and tread across centuries.

(1979)

White Night

A night of full moon
on a rooftop of this old city
I am reminded of a forest night
from many years ago.

When, under the moon,
the forest called out to forests,
and barasinghas called
to those left behind,
around desolate bends, among tall bushes,
while vanishing from view.

Does it all still remain?
The yellow-soiled paths and the hares,
the dense mahogany trees,
the fragrant, coarse grass,
the lingering twilight dew,
the caretaker's hut and
the seven stars above it.

In this urban night of the full moon,
why am I reminded of
the forest night?

I peer down from the roof—
midnight is shattering.

Moonlight scatters everywhere.

I am most drawn to the footpaths
the footpaths of midnight—
empty and open,
as if courtyards have stayed within me since childhood,
and open rooftops have called to me with the night,
no matter where I am.

What lies within this moonlit glow?
In this shattering midnight?
A helplessness
that tramples me, and a hope
that feels like unease.

We settled into the city
as if its foundation was laid on breaking apart family.
Neither our ancestors came with us,
nor the village, nor the animals.
What does it mean to settle in a city?
To be destroyed in it?

Images of a large refugee camp—
their futureless tents everywhere.
What kind of journey are we part of
that even now, our faces bear the mark of the displaced?

We merely call a city our own,
a house our own—
Yet, within these,
we continue to wander.

Very little of Lucknow remains in Lucknow,
very little of Allahabad in Allahabad,
or in Kanpur, Benaras, Patna and Aligarh—
In these cities,
many forms of violence, many kinds of markets, many types of traders.
Within them, around them,
far from them,
Bombay, Hyderabad, Amritsar,
and up to Srinagar—
violence
and the preparation of violence,
and the power of violence.

There are no dialogues, arguments—
murders happen.
And those arguments that continue,
also end in murders.

I, too, wanted to find meaning
in being born in India.
But even that India no longer exists,
the one in which I was born.

What is there in this full-moon light?
In this shattering midnight?
That my breath gets entangled
with Lahore, Karachi and Sindh?

Does Lahore remain?
What country is it in now?
Neither in India, nor in Pakistan,
neither in Urdu, nor in Punjabi.
Ask the nation-builders,
Did Lahore manage to settle again?

Like this untouchable
evening's white night
there is truth—
Lahore, too, is my truth.

Where is it,
that green-skied city of Baghdad?
Look for it.
where in Arabia is it now?

Ask the warlords,
on this whitening night,
Can they rebuild Baghdad?

They cannot even grow a date palm.
They cannot walk across the sand

as far as a camel calf can,
playing with dunes and dust
as if with the cosmos.

Can they create a camel?
A dome, a watermelon, a tall pitcher
a spring
that slowly turned into a stream?
An alley
that wound through the city under the shadows of high walls?
And in that alley,
a girl with a turquoise cloth on her head,
who will never again be seen in that alley.

Now, when you think of her,
she will return to memory.
Now, your memory is her Baghdad,
your memory is her alley, her lifetime,
her turquoise cloth
When Bhagat Singh walked towards the noose,
non-violence
was his concern.
If he had accepted
the justice of the warlords,
he, too, might have lived,
endured—
Dying slowly, every day,

like Lahore
like Benaras, Amritsar, Lucknow, Allahabad
Kanpur and Srinagar.

(1997)

Man of the Masses

Against the inhuman spark of an ice cutter
striking flesh like a human cutter,
my poem passes through burning villages;
amid fierce fire and piercing screams,
it first finds a charred woman.

In doing so, my poem sustains burns everywhere,
and even today, poems are used as hearses,
words are given oxygen of new phrases to breathe life.
But who is born in a curfew,
whose breath burns as hot as loo winds,
that young miner's mind
remembers my poem like a brand-new gun!

When I entered, with millions of people,
into the forbidden land of poetry.
It was a vulgar disruption
to all those poets
who, for their own comfort,
soaked their Sundays in opium water.
Now, my poem cries out—like a life being taken
not with language or rhythm, but with meaning—
beside that a pregnant woman,

her stomach shot,
so no honest person would ever be born.

While swallowing rotten rats,
their throats choked on time.
Eyes hardened with patches of dead memories,
they retreat into forests forever,
evading people.
For in the thinnest vein of their thigh,
words begin;
in the thickest vein, they end.
They mask their intentions in the freshness of language,
just for the sake of an argument,
they take names of places like Srikakulam.
They have become strangely successful in this country,
calling the living
by the names of dead.

These professional murderers
strangle naked news
behind sensational newspaper headlines.
Tamed by the faces
whose toilet plans are bigger than the map of my village.

Publishing houses in this country,
like leeches found in icy cracks.
Before dying by suicide on the banks of Hooghly
why did the young poet shout 'Times of India'—

It was impossible for me to see his dead body.
Even a hired mourner couldn't weep for him.
Because today, before anything else,
he must strike with his true strength!

Every time I write a poem,
I'm faced with explosive grief—
that, for how long must I carry
this wretched map of the world?
That, in millions of villages bound
by the chains of battle tanks,
for how long must a person sleep and tarry?

In the Calcutta zoo, a rhino once said to me—
Freedom is nowhere; everywhere there's security.
In the capital's safest quarters,
a primal wound festers,
that, with the help of wild cats, births a beastly separation.
Ever since then, I have decided
that rhinoceros' tough skin must not be used for war
but for boundless compassion.

Right now, I am reading alphabets carved on flesh—
equipped with toxic gases and dangerous spies,
a lowly hand in this system,
breaks into my house at any time.
And with electric whips,
strips my mother's thighs,

my sister's back,
my daughter's chest.
Before my eyes,
he destroys everything—
from my vote to my reproductive power.
Tied by rope around my waist,
I'm dragged across,
while the whole village
witnesses the gruesome scene
like mere spectators.
For, until now, poems have only been written
about being jailed,
but never about blowing up a jail for the right person.

One evening,
as I searched for fresh, fiery words—
thousands of babies, born last Sunday, soundly slept.
Their height
just a little taller than my pen that writes poetry.
Then, in a corner, I spotted them—they were standing upright,
like loaded guns, like sirens, like white cheetahs,
like curriculum, like stench, like the Constitution.
They stood like guardians,
beyond my reach—cruel parasites.
For them, I was unarmed,
because words cannot harm them,

so long as seven-centimetre-long bullets
remain loaded in rifles, ready to fire.
They will take these children
from their cradles straight to the armouries.
They will do everything
to make sure these children never meet me,
for our meeting will set fire to the armouries.

I descended like the sound of deep waters.
Outside, in the air, on the streets,
fire-engine drivers caught hold of me and asked—
If this continues, what will be the future of words?
For how long will we be remembered only for running fire-engines?
Meanwhile, Dom youths went on strike—
saying they will no longer just cremate
the bodies of those who died young
but will also visit the homes of the dead.

Often, while writing poetry,
my knee knocks against the boat of an unnamed sailor,
and the search for a new country begins—
It isn't necessary for that country to be called Vietnam,
it could also bear the name of my father, who was swept away in the floods,
or the name of my village,
or that threshing ground
where I have long been auctioning off my crops and my lines!

Why did an old neighbour ask—
I am a landless farmer,
can I touch poetry?
Those with young chests and strong shoulders,
whose blood burns in mica mines
never even once in their lives
think of mica as 'mica'.
Why is it that every time,
the question of poetry is left out from the question of common lives?

In history, since primal times,
the spaces emptied in the name of poetry—
lately, only boxes filled with fat have been collected there.
The writhing, 21-foot-long intestine of Sukanta
has been extracted and placed inside a deep-blue glass,
not to germinate the spine of eternal rebellion,
but to make the museum of poetry
even more bizarre.
Among fine-tobacco-like poems
that gather a horde of unsuccessful, old lovers,
my shepherd-like face, steeped in sheep scent,
must have been unexpected for all of you—
as unexpected as the corpse of Gajanan Madhav Muktibodh
floating, like fish, inside the glass tank of a Jain merchant.

Why do my poems bear the face of those affected by a bomb blast?
Why can't I write poems

like children's sleep,
like a mine,
like the colour of ripe jamun?
Why can't I write poems
like the scent of new hay on a mother's body,
like the musk of a deer's in a bamboo forest,
like a rabbit's ears,
like the mating of blue water birds
in the desolate solitude of summer,
like the briny, reddish-brown depths of the oceanic caverns?
Why can't I write poems
like the back of a waterfall plunging from thousands of feet above?
A poem, written in grave letters, as deep as an elephant's footprints—
one carved into walls,
etched onto millions of ploughs,
cold and stretched thin,
like feeble roti in tiffin carriers
of countless farmers?
Their poems had been battling a dead bear.
Those gamblers who have turned poetry into horse racing—
their bets can be broken
only by the one you call a common man,
for he is greater than any nation's flag.
He has begun to feel it,
he has begun to sense

the hundreds of novels written upon his back,
the canals and roads carved by his own hands.

This is the great possibility of poetry—
that the common man has begun to feel his own creations.
He has begun to sense
the metropolises balanced on his legs,
the capital cities resting on his waist.
Slowly, his face is changing.
He has begun to feel
the gleaming, claw-like blade of the plough,
the true relationship between seed, water and land.

Expanding the meaning of poetry,
he unleashes words like sniffer dogs,
glimpsing, within a scattered moment,
the loneliness of chains.
He knows—
why an adivasi child stares at the alphabet,
fearful even of script,
as it reveals the secrets of the most sickening book of history.

(1972)

Bruno's Daughters

They were not made of sackcloth or moss.
They had mothers,
and they themselves were mothers.

They had names,
names they were called since childhood,
until the day of the murder,
even by those
who killed them.

They had faces,
they had bodies, they had hair
and shadows in sunlight.

In the fields near the Ganges, they had their hours of work
for which they had to be paid wages every time!
The way Earth had to be seen
through Galileo's telescope.

They were not ashes or lies.
They were mothers.
And says who? Who? What beast?
that they gave birth outside their will?

Their pregnancy was not apathy,
not a mistake,

not a habit—
their pregnancy was not an addiction or an assault.

Who says so?
Which economist?
They had lovers.
There was sound that ringed inside them.

They were mothers.
They too had nine months—
not inside the belly of a whale, but in the whole world,
nine months of the whole world.

The world is whole and unbroken,
it cannot be isolated from anything,
then why this desolate hunting of motherhood?

You never wanted
the whole world to enter the village
where those women labourers were killed?

What citizenship do they hold
when all evidence of their existence has been erased?
Until last evening,
until midnight,
they were part of Earth's population—
just like the Earth itself,
just like their killers.

But this morning?
When they were burned alive last night?

Does the world of the living
rest solely on the living?

Even this morning, they remain part of the Earth's population.

They have friends,
they have their poets
and their failures—
which have shaped Indian time.

It is not just their class that defines their time!

By tomorrow evening, this scorched land
will glow like an unbaked earthen lamp
and
summon its new inhabitants.

They were not nomads.
The wells bear the marks of their earthen pots,
the pale trunks of rosewood
carry the scars of their axes.
The stones they placed,
to descend the dam's slopes
still remain.

Their everyday footsteps have carved paths in the soil.

They did not appear out of nowhere.
They arrived here,
walking along the shores of blue.

They had doors,
through which cradles could be seen,
and colourful ribbons for tying hair,
papaya trees,
freshly cut grass
and tobacco leaves,
drying slowly,
and a spear for killing snakes.

They were not stains or noise.
They had lamps,
pets,
homes.

They had homes
where split chickpeas simmered slowly over the fire,
where dough was kneaded,
the salt stored in earthen pots
seeping out during the monsoon.
They had homes
that lay in the paths of wandering cats.

Night fell there.
The moon became round.

There were walls.
They had courtyards,
where straw flew in the air
to be caught by birds.

There was imagination.
There was memory.

There were walls
bearing the marks of clouds and horns.
There were walls
that kept shrubs
from entering the courtyards.

The walls of a home
built on a concrete desire to settle down.
They had shaped them from wet lumps of soil—
not from a porcupine's quills,
not with a bear's claws.

Which scoundrel shows them as jungles
framed on colourful screens through a camera?

They were walls of clay,
not prehistoric rocks.
Every year, they were coated with fresh clay.
These were their homes—not a waiting,
not the hollows of trees,
not an eagle's claws clutching a rat.

Their homes were not inside lion's jaws.
They had a fixed place on the map—
whole and complete.

They came to work so early in the morning
that their sarees were soaked with dew,
damp with the glow of a sinking moon.

They came so early in the morning—
Where did they come from? Where did they arrive?
Why did they come so early?
For which country did they come to so early in the morning?

Did they come so early in the morning
only for their masters?
Not for me?
Not for you?

Was their early morning arrival
only to feed their families?
How do you view this labour?
The oil well being drilled in the Indian Ocean—
is it outside my life?
Is it merely a government project?

How do you view this labour!

They did not call cities betrayals or traps.

Cities were not just prisons or lost legal battles to them.

They saw cities,
not with the eyes of wild animals.

Cities came and went in their lives—
not merely as possessions or systems of law,
but mostly with their sons,
who, even now,
can be seen toiling around the kilns.

They were murdered.
They did not die by suicide.
The significance and remembrance of this fact
will never fade from poetry.

What was within their being
that they were burnt alive?
In the final years of the twentieth century,
in a country
that has a parliament?

What was within their being
that could not be bought,
that could not be used?

That which had to be annihilated by fire—
and that too, at midnight,
surrounded by cowards with guns?

I keep repeating myself.
I am proclaiming a simple truth on a grand scale.

My everything depends
on this simple truth.

What was within their being
that even fire could not destroy?

Their paths were not wild swords,
their people did not vanish like kings—
the masters of blind canons and mad elephants
turned to fossils while still alive.

But those who tilled with wooden ploughs
still continue.

Queens vanished.
Their memory—worth less
than a rusted tin can.

Queens vanished.
But women,
reaping to the horizon,
continue to reap.

(1989)

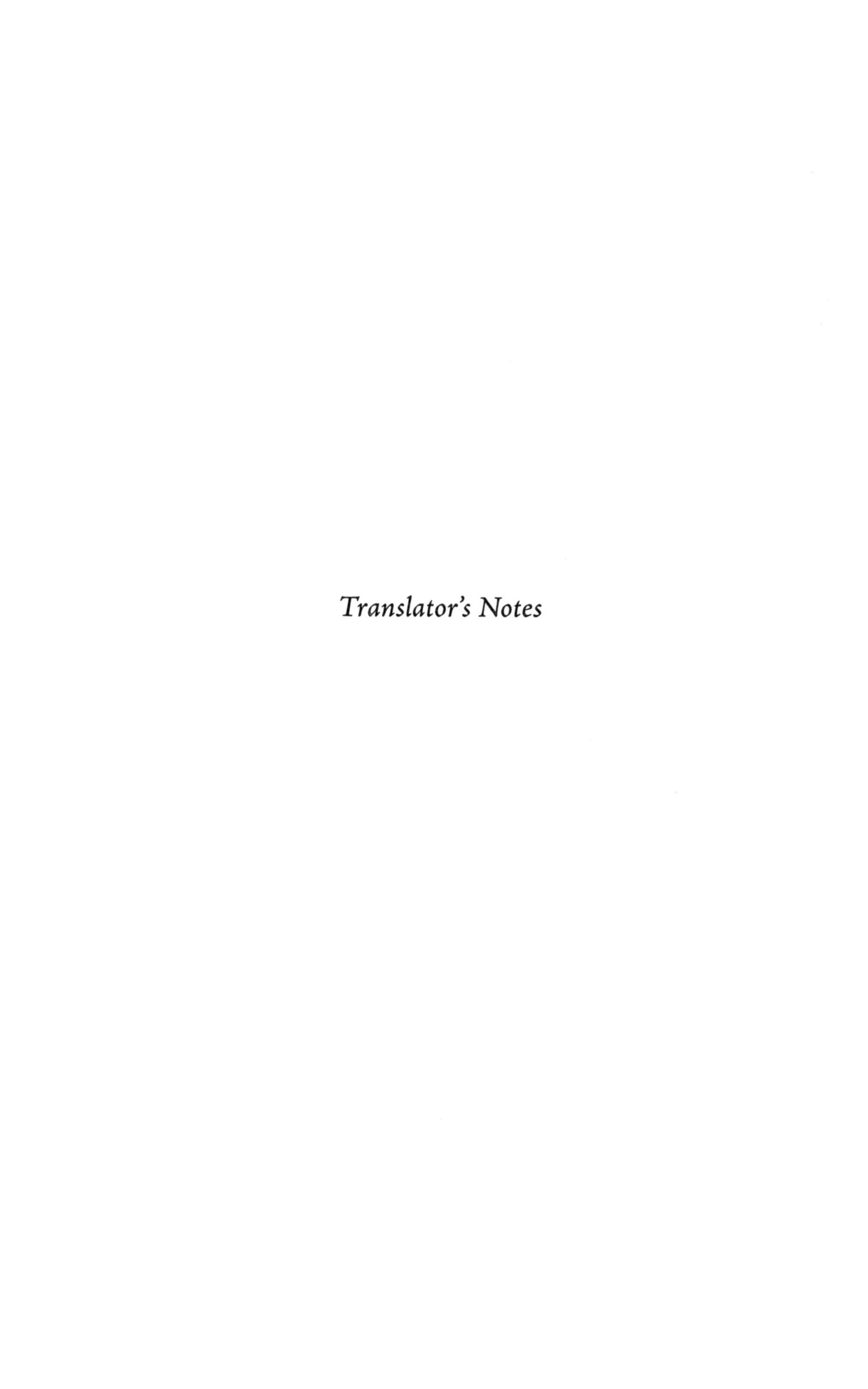

Translator's Notes

PAGE *v* | **Gyanranjan,** born in 1936, is a renowned Hindi writer and professor who has authored several popular short story collections, many of which have been translated into multiple languages. He has received numerous prestigious awards for his literary contributions and remains a key figure in Indian literature and the progressive writers' movement.

PAGE 4 | **'Ichamati and Meghna . . . Ghaghara',** the seven major rivers—spanning India, Pakistan and Bangladesh—are vital lifelines of the subcontinent, shaping its geography, culture and history.

PAGE 8 | The poem invokes **Mir Taqi Mir** (1723–1810), one of the most renowned Urdu poets of the eighteenth century. His poetry, marked by deep melancholy and themes of love, loss and Sufism, profoundly influenced Urdu literature. His magnum opus, *Nikāt ush-Shu'arā,* is considered a foundational work on Urdu poetics.

PAGE 8 | **janab,** a respectful Urdu honorific, often used to address someone with esteem or fondness.

PAGE 11 | **'Holding new tongs . . . Eidgah fair',** alludes to the short story 'Eidgah' by Munshi Premchand, about a little boy named Hamid and his selfless act of love for his grandmother.

PAGE 11 | On **6 December** 1992, the Babri Masjid was demolished by a mob of Hindu right-wing extremists in Ayodhya, Uttar Pradesh.

PAGE 39 | ***Awara*** and ***Shri 420*** are classic 1950s Hindi films directed by Raj Kapoor, who also stars as the protagonist. Both films explore themes of class struggle and social justice. The songs composed by Shankar–Jaikishan and Kapoor's portrayal of the 'tramp' persona became iconic in popular culture.

PAGE 39 | **lafanga**, a colloquial Hindi term used to describe someone as a loafer, vagabond or troublemaker.

PAGE 40 | **chowk**, a bustling public square or marketplace, often serves as the heart of social and commercial life in towns and cities across the Indian Subcontinent.

PAGE 43 | A version of the poem 'Patang' (Kite) is included in the NCERT Hindi curriculum for higher-secondary students.

PAGE 44 | **nagada**, a traditional Indian kettle drum, typically played in pairs with sticks, used in folk and ceremonial music.

PAGE 45 | **mridanga**, a barrel-shaped percussion instrument that features prominently in devotional and folk traditions of Hindustani music, as well as in Carnatic music.

PAGE 51 | **basti** refers to an informal settlement or neighbourhood; the term is often used in the context of urban slums.

PAGE 60 | **dupatta**, a long scarf worn by women in South Asia, typically as part of traditional attire such as the salwar kameez.

PAGE 60 | **santoor**, a stringed instrument, played with lightweight wooden mallets, known for its delicate, shimmering notes.

PAGE 61 | **'the month of March'** marks the beginning of the wedding season, coinciding with auspicious dates in the Hindu calendar following the end of winter and the onset of spring.

PAGE 78 | ***The Times of India***, one of India's oldest and most widely circulated English-language newspapers, has played a key role in India's colonial and post-independence media landscape and is known for its wide-ranging coverage of politics, business and culture.

PAGE **81** | **Dom**, a historically marginalized community in India, traditionally associated with cremation work and manual scavenging, have long been subjected to social exclusion under the oppressively hierarchical caste system.

PAGE **82** | **Sukanta** (1926–1947) was a Bengali poet known for his poignant and revolutionary verses, often addressing themes of social justice, youth and resistance. Despite his early death, his powerful poems continue to inspire generations of readers and activists.

PAGE **82** | **Gajanan Madhav Muktibodh** (1917–1968) was a prominent Hindi poet and thinker, recognized for his profound, introspective poetry that explored existential questions and social issues. He died in relative obscurity after a prolonged illness, but his work gained wide recognition after his death.

PAGE **85** | The title of the poem invokes **Giordano Filippo Bruno**, the sixteenth-century Italian philosopher and cosmological theorist who challenged the authority of the Church and its religious dogma by supporting Copernicus' heliocentric model. In 1600, he was burned alive by the Roman Inquisition. Years later, astronomer Galileo provided empirical evidence supporting heliocentrism.